Canadian Writing Series

PARAGRAPH
WRITING
GRADE 2 TO 4

Written by Marie-Helen Goyetche

200 Writing Prompts! This book provides a step-by step method to teach paragraph writing. Students will learn and practise how to write the different parts that make a paragraph. Models and practise worksheets cover topic sentences, paragraph details, and the concluding sentence. An over view of the Trait-Based Writing is included. 40 weeks of paragraph prompts help students master their paragraph writing skills.

Marie-Helen Goyetche is an elementary school principal and freelance writer. Marie-Helen received her Bachelors in Education from Concordia University and her Masters in Educational Leadership from Bishops University. She has over 100 articles and over 40 curriculum books published.

Published in Canada by:
On The Mark Press
15 Dairy Avenue, Napanee, Ontario, K7R 1M4
www.onthemarkpress.com

Funded by the
Government
of Canada

Canada

 R1155 ISBN: 978-1-4877-0442-1 © On The Mark Press

At A Glance

In this book you will find how to introduce, explain and practise:

Writing Topic Sentences
Writing Details
Writing Concluding Sentences
Para-jamble activities
200+ Paragraph prompts
Paragraph of the Week Worksheet

  R1155 ISBN: 978-1-4877-0442-1 © On The Mark Press

Table of Contents

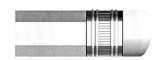

How to use this book

In this book you will find:

● An overview of the Trait-Based Writing.

● Writing Task Rubrics for both teacher and student to use based on the Trait-Based Writing.

● A teacher/peer and student writing checklist to work on between the draft and good copy.

● An explanation to give students on how-to write a paragraph.

● Use the step-by step method of writing a paragraph and the different parts: topic sentence, details, concluding sentence, and the paragraph parts in the right sequence.

● A blank Paragraph of the Week where the students could brainstorm different subject ideas on what they would like to write about.

● A blank Paragraph of the Week worksheet (reproducible).

● 40 weeks (5 prompts per subject = 200 prompts) paragraph of the week (day) prompts.

● A tip sheet how to create a Writing Centre.

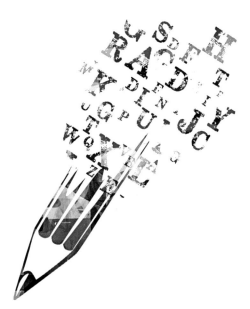

● Laminate the how-to write a paragraph for visual support to students.

This book is fully reproducible. It is recommended to make photocopies of the worksheets to be placed at the Writing Centre.

R1155 ISBN: 978-1-4877-0442-1 © On The Mark Press

Organization

- Sequencing
- Using beginning, middle and end
- Writing a complete piece
- Logical order
- Transition

Voice

- Looking at Point-of-view
- Choosing right point-of-view for the right purpose
- Using different voices
- Using own words

Ideas

- Good knowledge of topic
- Stays on topic
- Elaborating and developing ideas on topic
- Is specific on topic

Conventions

- Writes clear sentences (no run-ons) mechanics of writing
- Uses punctuation
- Spelling
- Grammar

Word Choice & Details

- Using action words
- Adding and using descriptive words (Adjectives and Adverbs)
- The details are staying on topic
- Using expressions the audience will understand

Sentence Fluency

- Flowing sentences
- Smooth paragraph
- Use of short and long sentences

Teacher Rubric Evaluation: Writing Tasks

Name of Student: _____   Title:_____

	1	2	3	4
Beginning Middle End (Organization)	The sentences are not in any order	There is some attempt at Beginning/Middle/End	Beginning/Middle/End are all present	Interesting and complete Beginning/Middle/End
Ideas	The main idea is not clear	The idea needs to be worked on	There is one main idea	There is one main idea and sub (ideas)
Details	Details need to be added	More details are needed	You have many details	You have many excellent details
Word Choice	The same words are used over and over again	You use one or two new words	You used many new words and expressions	Excellent vocabulary
Sentence Fluency	The piece does not make sense	The piece is somewhat clear	The piece is clear	The piece is clear, and the audience is targeted
Voice	The piece does not have a voice	The piece has somewhat a voice	The voice matches the purpose of the text	Point of view is clear and maintained
Conventions	Too many spelling & grammatical errors, text doesn't make sense	There are some spelling and grammatical errors	There are few spelling and grammatical errors	Spelling, grammar and mechanics of writing are clear
Creativity	No creativity is shown in the piece	There is an attempt made to be creative	There is some creativity and originality	Very creative and original

Student Self-Evaluation Rubric Evaluation: Writing Tasks

Name of Student: _____   Title:_____

	1	2	3	4
Beginning Middle End (Organization)	My sentences are not in any order	I have made an attempt to include a Beginning/Middle/End	I wrote a clear Beginning/Middle/End	I wrote an interesting and complete Beginning/Middle/End
Ideas	What is my main idea?	My idea needs to be worked on	I have one main idea	I have one main idea and some sub (ideas)
Details	I don't have any details	I needs to add more details	I have many details	I have many excellent details
Word Choice	I use the same words over and over again	I added one or two new words	I added many new words and expressions	I added difficult and well-chosen words
Clearness	My work does not make sense	My work is somewhat clear	My work is clear	My work is clear, and I know who my audience is
Voice	My piece does not have a voice	My piece has somewhat a voice	My voice matches the purpose of the text	My Point of View is clear and maintained
Conventions	Too many spelling & grammatical errors, my text doesn't make sense	There are some spelling and grammatical errors	There are few spelling and grammatical errors	Spelling, grammar and mechanics of writing are clear
Creativity	I do not show creativity	I have made an attempt to show creativity	I have shown some creativity and originality	I have clearly shown creativity and originality

   R1155 ISBN: 978-1-4877-0442-1 © On The Mark Press

Teacher/Peer Writing Checklist

Title:_____ Written by: _____

Feedback by:_____

1	There is a good sentence for the beginning paragraph.	
2	There are sentences used in the body of the piece.	
3	There is a good ending sentence.	
4	The idea is present and clear.	
5	The message is clear.	
6	The writing category is clear	
7	The sentences are clear and well placed into paragraphs.	
8	There are new and some difficult words used.	
9	There is no repetition.	
10	Capitals, periods and punctuation have been checked.	
11	The piece flows well when read aloud.	
12	The good copy is ready to be written.	

Student Writing Checklist

Title:_____ Written by: _____

1	I have a good sentence for the beginning paragraph.	
2	I have used sentences in the body of my work.	
3	I included a good ending sentence.	
4	My idea is present and clear.	
5	My message is clear.	
6	The writing category is clear.	
7	My sentences are clear and well placed into paragraphs.	
8	I have used new and some difficult words.	
9	I don't repeat.	
10	I have checked for capitals, periods and punctuation.	
11	My piece flows well when I read it aloud.	
12	I am ready now do my good copy.	

HOW TO WRITE A PARAGRAPH

When writing a complete paragraph, there are a few important details you need to include.

Title: You will need a great title to peak your readers curiosity.

Topic Sentence: This will clarify and narrow your subject and will open up your paragraph.

Details: Great paragraphs have 3 to 5 supporting details that further explain your topic sentence.

Concluding Sentence: This sentence will close your paragraph and should be similar and support your topic sentence.

_____

title

Topic sentence

_____

Detail 1

_____

Detail 2

_____

Detail 3

_____

Detail 4

_____

Detail 5

_____

Concluding sentence

_____

   R1155 ISBN: 978-1-4877-0442-1 © On The Mark Press

Read the paragraph below and write the topic of the paragraph on the line.

Illustrate the story in the box.

Today was a great day to go to the zoo! The weather was perfect. Not too hot. Not too cold. The sun was shining. There were some people but there weren't any big crowds. The animals were outside soaking in the sun too. We followed the zookeepers as they fed the animals. It was a perfect day to see the animals at the zoo.

Topic: _____

My mom and I baked a cake. Every once in a while, my mother always takes out her great, big, recipe book. She makes a list of ingredients she is missing and then we go grocery shopping. Once we get back home, we put the groceries away and set the ingredients aside on the counter. The most fun of all is I get to lick the spoon. I love baking cakes with my mom.

Topic: _____

 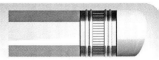

Read the paragraph below and write the topic of the paragraph on the line.

Illustrate the story in the box.

My favourite author is Dr. Seuss. I love the story of The Lorax. On Sunday morning, my dad reads us Green Eggs and Ham. At Christmas time my grandfather reads How the Grinch stole Christmas. My cousin can read Horton Hears A Who! over and over and over again. My all-time favourite is The Cat in the Hat. I love all his books. I love Theodor Seuss Geisel.

Topic: _____

Julie and I love to draw together. After school, she comes over and we bring our markers and our fancy paper out to the table. We draw different objects that we like with our markers, but we don't colour the inside, we only draw the outline. We use our colouring pencils or wax crayons or sometimes our pastels. Then we colour inside the lines and add colour to our drawings. Julie and I are artists who love to draw.

Topic: _____

    R1155 ISBN: 978-1-4877-0442-1 © On The Mark Press

Read the paragraph below and write the topic of the paragraph on the line.

Illustrate the story in the box.

I would like to build a house out of blocks. I have many, many blocks. I can use the big blocks to create the walls. I can use the medium sized blocks to create the furniture. I can use the small blocks to build accessories that belong in the house. I have enough blocks to make the rows in different colours and I would then have a striped house. One day, I will build a house using blocks.

Topic: _____

I love to build sand castles. I take my pail, fill it to the brim with sand and pack it down hard. Then carefully place them upside down so the sand stays together. I build the walls of my castle with many upside-down pails. Then I use an empty drinking cup and fill it with sand to the brim. I flip many of them over the layer underneath. I then build layer over layer. I use miniature glasses to build another layer on top of the medium layer. I use straws, wooden sticks and shells to decorate my sand castle. I wish I could be small enough to live in a sand castle.

Topic: _____

R1155 ISBN: 978-1-4877-0442-1 © On The Mark Press

WRITE THE TOPIC SENTENCE

Look carefully at the picture(s) in each box. Write a topic sentence that goes along with the picture.

Topic Sentence:

_____

Topic Sentence:

_____

Topic Sentence:

_____

R1155 ISBN: 978-1-4877-0442-1 © On The Mark Press

WRITE THE TOPIC SENTENCE

Look carefully at the picture(s) in each box. Write a topic sentence that goes along with the picture.

Topic Sentence:

_____

Topic Sentence:

_____

Topic Sentence:

_____

WRITE THE TOPIC SENTENCE

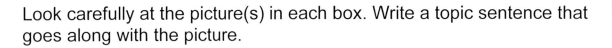

Look carefully at the picture(s) in each box. Write a topic sentence that goes along with the picture.

Topic Sentence:

_____

Topic Sentence:

_____

Topic Sentence:

_____

 R1155 ISBN: 978-1-4877-0442-1 © On The Mark Press

WRITE THE TOPIC SENTENCE

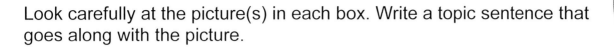

Look carefully at the picture(s) in each box. Write a topic sentence that goes along with the picture.

Topic Sentence:

_____

Topic Sentence:

_____

Topic Sentence:

_____

WHAT'S THE TOPIC SENTENCE?

Read the paragraph below. Write an appropriate topic sentence to match the paragraph. Draw a picture to match the paragraph.

My mom dresses me and my sister warmly to go play in the snow. We play together and make many, many, many snowballs. Some snowballs are big and some are small. We place them one on top of each other to create walls. My favourite part is to pretend that we are building our houses and my sister's favourite part is to sit there and eat the snow. We love playing outside in the winter.

Topic sentence:

_____

Draw your topic.

R1155 ISBN: 978-1-4877-0442-1 © On The Mark Press

WHAT'S THE TOPIC SENTENCE?

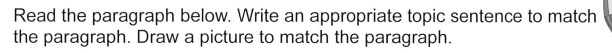

Read the paragraph below. Write an appropriate topic sentence to match the paragraph. Draw a picture to match the paragraph.

Our family's bedtime routine is very easy. After bath time, we get into our pajamas. We run to the bathroom to brush our teeth. Then we comb our hair. We run back to our bedroom and climb into one bed. Dad squeezes in-between me and my brother. Dad reads us a bedtime story. He is so good at it, most of the time we beg him for another one. Some nights he says yes and other nights we go back to our own bed after one story. I am happy my dad reads to me before going to bed.

Topic sentence:

_____

Draw your topic.

WHAT'S THE TOPIC SENTENCE?

Read the paragraph below. Write an appropriate topic sentence to match the paragraph. Draw a picture to match the paragraph.

My school holds a book fair twice a year. We usually go home after school and have supper. After supper instead of getting ready for bed, we put on our jackets and get into the car. Back to school we go. There are many books there. Science books, poetry books, craft books, cooking books. We can also find comic books. I spend the money I have been collecting since the last book fair. I always look forward to the school book fairs.

Topic sentence:

_____

Draw your topic.

R1155 ISBN: 978-1-4877-0442-1 © On The Mark Press

NOW LET'S GET TO THE NITTY GRITTY!

Read the topic sentence and concluding sentence below. Be creative and write three to five details to go along with the topic sentence and concluding sentence. Give your paragraph a title.

_____

title

Topic sentence: One morning, as I woke up I fell out of bed.

_____

_____

_____

_____

_____

Concluding sentence: That was a horrible day!

Draw your topic.

NOW LET'S GET TO THE NITTY GRITTY!

Read the topic sentence and concluding sentence below. Be creative and write three to five details to go along with the topic sentence and concluding sentence. Give your paragraph a title.

_____

title

Topic sentence: One day, it snowed like crazy!

_____

_____

_____

_____

Concluding sentence: We had so much fun in the snow.

Draw your topic.

┌───┐
│   │
│   │
│   │
│   │
│   │
│   │
│   │
│   │
└───┘

  R1155 ISBN: 978-1-4877-0442-1 © On The Mark Press

NOW LET'S GET TO THE NITTY GRITTY!

Read the topic sentence and concluding sentence below. Be creative and write three to five details to go along with the topic sentence and concluding sentence. Give your paragraph a title.

_____

title

Topic sentence: My second home is grandma's place.

_____

_____

_____

_____

Concluding sentence: I'm happy at grandma's.

Draw your topic.

NOW LET'S GET TO THE NITTY GRITTY!

Read the topic sentence and concluding sentence below. Be creative and write three to five details to go along with the topic sentence and concluding sentence. Give your paragraph a title.

_____

title

Topic sentence: You shouldn't share your computer password.

_____

_____

_____

_____

_____

Concluding sentence: Now you know why you keep your password private.

Draw your topic.

R1155 ISBN: 978-1-4877-0442-1 © On The Mark Press

NOW LET'S GET TO THE NITTY GRITTY!

Read the topic sentence and concluding sentence below. Be creative and write three to five details to go along with the topic sentence and concluding sentence. Give your paragraph a title.

_____

title

Topic sentence: A vegetarian omelette – my favourite!

_____

_____

_____

_____

_____

Concluding sentence: I love eating omelettes on the weekend!

Draw your topic.

NOW LET'S GET TO THE NITTY GRITTY!

Read the topic sentence and concluding sentence below. Be creative and write three to five details to go along with the topic sentence and concluding sentence. Give your paragraph a title.

_____

title

Topic sentence: I write in my agenda every day!

_____

_____

_____

_____

_____

Concluding sentence: Now I never forget my homework or special events.

Draw your topic.

_____

 R1155 ISBN: 978-1-4877-0442-1 © On The Mark Press

NOW LET'S GET TO THE NITTY GRITTY!

Read the topic sentence and concluding sentence below. Be creative and write three to five details to go along with the topic sentence and concluding sentence. Give your paragraph a title.

_____

title

Topic sentence: I read a story book every night at bedtime.

_____

_____

_____

_____

Concluding sentence: I am a good reader because I read often.

Draw your topic.

WRITE THE CONCLUDING SENTENCE

Read the topic sentence and paragraph below. Write a concluding sentence to go along with the topic sentence and paragraph. Give your paragraph a title.

_____

title

The best summer vacation ever was 2 years ago. I went camping in Wasaga Beach. I swam in the pool. I had pizza every Friday night. I played on the beach and in the playground. I went boat riding.

Concluding Sentence: _____

_____

· ·

_____

title

My favourite season is summer. I love summer because my birthday is in July. I play soccer in the city league. The weather is hot. I wear shorts, a t-shirt and flip-flops all summer long.

Concluding Sentence: _____

_____

R1155 ISBN: 978-1-4877-0442-1 © On The Mark Press

WRITE THE CONCLUDING SENTENCE

Read the topic sentence and paragraph below. Write a concluding sentence to go along with the topic sentence and paragraph. Give your paragraph a title.

_____

title

We had a great time on New Year's Eve. We ate finger foods. We played games. We wore pointed looking hats. We blew into funny horns. We counted down the last ten seconds of the year.

Concluding Sentence: _____

_____

. . . .

_____

title

I love candies! On Halloween, I dressed up like a Power Ranger. I had lots of fun while trick or treating. I also went to the school Halloween dance. I danced and ran around with Billy who was also dressed as a Power Ranger.

Concluding Sentence: _____

_____

R1155 ISBN: 978-1-4877-0442-1 © On The Mark Press

WRITE THE CONCLUDING SENTENCE

Read the topic sentence and paragraph below. Write a concluding sentence to go along with the topic sentence and paragraph. Give your paragraph a title.

_____

title

For my party, the Serpent man came to my house. We saw many giant pythons and snakes. We petted a lizard. We touched a turtle. The Serpent man put a huge snake on my mom's shoulders and she wasn't scared.

Concluding Sentence: _____

_____

. . . .

_____

title

I love winter! I can do so many things outside during the winter. I can play hockey. I can go sliding. I can go skiing. My dad will show me how to snowboard soon. I love to play in the snow. The weather is cold. Sometimes it is very cold so I wear a hat, scarf, mitts, a jacket and snow pants.

Concluding Sentence: _____

_____

R1155 ISBN: 978-1-4877-0442-1 © On The Mark Press

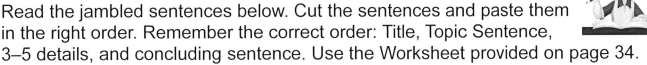

Read the jambled sentences below. Cut the sentences and paste them in the right order. Remember the correct order: Title, Topic Sentence, 3–5 details, and concluding sentence. Use the Worksheet provided on page 34.

I also have a netted cage.

Butterflies

I have a butterfly net.

Next summer, not only will I catch butterflies but I will take pictures of them before I let them go.

I love to chase and catch butterflies.

During the summer, I love to catch butterflies.

I never keep them for very long.

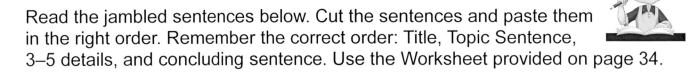

Read the jambled sentences below. Cut the sentences and paste them in the right order. Remember the correct order: Title, Topic Sentence, 3–5 details, and concluding sentence. Use the Worksheet provided on page 34.

When I help mom bake cookies, I measure the ingredients,

I measure the dry ingredients.

I measure the wet ingredients.

I tell mom when the timer goes off.

I stir everything together.

Chocolate chip cookies

When I help mom bake, she also make me clean the dishes.

R1155 ISBN: 978-1-4877-0442-1 © On The Mark Press

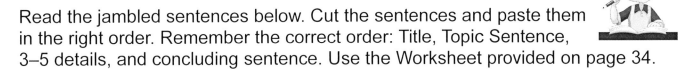

Read the jambled sentences below. Cut the sentences and paste them in the right order. Remember the correct order: Title, Topic Sentence, 3–5 details, and concluding sentence. Use the Worksheet provided on page 34.

I have clothes all over my floor.

I have many things in my room.

My room needs to be cleaned up.

In My Room

My desk is covered with books.

My room is really messy.

My shelves are overflowing.

I don't remember the colour of my carpet.

PARA-JAMBLE

Read the jambled sentences below. Cut the sentences and paste them in the right order. Remember the correct order: Title, Topic Sentence, 3–5 details, and concluding sentence. Use the Worksheet provided on page 34.

I want to cook for my family and I will take care of them.

I need to grow some more.

I want to drive a red pick-up truck.

I want to travel all over the world.

When I am older I want to be a veterinarian.

When I am older.

R1155 ISBN: 978-1-4877-0442-1 © On The Mark Press

PARA-JAMBLE

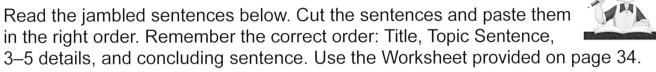

Read the jambled sentences below. Cut the sentences and paste them in the right order. Remember the correct order: Title, Topic Sentence, 3–5 details, and concluding sentence. Use the Worksheet provided on page 34.

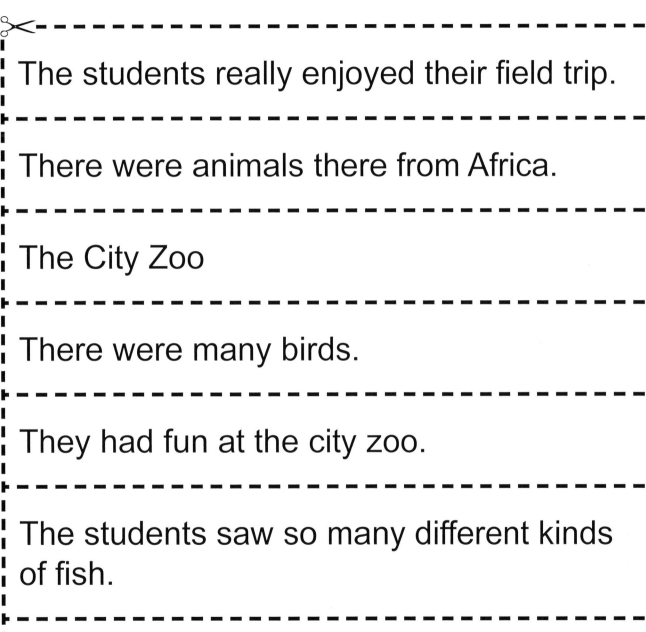

The students really enjoyed their field trip.

There were animals there from Africa.

The City Zoo

There were many birds.

They had fun at the city zoo.

The students saw so many different kinds of fish.

They saw the elephants and the lions.

title
topic sentence
detail
detail
detail
detail
detail
concluding sentence

   R1155 ISBN: 978-1-4877-0442-1 © On The Mark Press

IS IT? OR IS IT NOT?

Read the paragraph below. Answer the questions provided based on the paragraph you have just read.

Yesterday I went to Bob's birthday party. He had his party at his house. He invited many children from school. During the party, he opened his presents. We ate chicken nuggets, cake and drank lots of juice. I gave Bob a toy truck. We had a great time at Bob's birthday party.

1. Is the topic about presents? _____

2. There are five details about the party? _____

3. The topic sentence includes the theme of the party? _____

4. The kids didn't have a good time? _____

5. The party was a long time ago? _____

6. Record two other details you would add if this was your paragraph.

_____

_____

_____

IS IT? OR IS IT NOT?

Read the paragraph below. Answer the questions provided based on the paragraph you have just read.

Ice Cream Cones are the best! Although there are many different kinds of ice cream, my favourite flavour is vanilla. I like to dribble a little maple syrup on my cone. Then I like to sprinkle little candies on top. I don't add nuts on top because my brother is allergic to them. The best part about the cone is the sugar cone!!

1. Is the topic about candies? _____

2. There are five details about the ice cream cone? _____

3. The topic sentence describes the ice cream? _____

4. Is the allergy an important detail? _____

5. The topic sentence and the concluding sentence work together?

_____

6. Record two other details you would add if this was your paragraph.

_____

_____

_____

R1155 ISBN: 978-1-4877-0442-1 © On The Mark Press

PARAGRAPH WRITING:

A **paragraph** is made up of at least **5** complete and independent sentences. A paragraph is like a sandwich. Starting with a **topic sentence** that introduces your reader to what the paragraph will be about. The **middle** is made up of 3–5 supporting independent sentences. The **ending** has a concluding sentence that wraps up the topic.

EXAMPLE:

TOPIC	My favourite book
TOPIC SENTENCE	Let me tell you about my favourite book.
SUPPORTING SENTENCE	It has witches and wizards and lots of monsters.
SUPPORTING SENTENCE	The book takes place in a school for young witches and wizards.
SUPPORTING SENTENCE	At the school they get to practise magic and learn about monsters.
CLOSING SENTENCE	I wish I could go to a school that teaches magic.

TOPIC	What I know about Oranges.
TOPIC SENTENCE	
SUPPORTING SENTENCE	
SUPPORTING SENTENCE	
SUPPORTING SENTENCE	
CLOSING SENTENCE	

Draw your subject.

   R1155 ISBN: 978-1-4877-0442-1 © On The Mark Press

LET'S TRY A FEW PARAGRAPHS:

TOPIC	My favourite game.
TOPIC SENTENCE	_____ _____
SUPPORTING SENTENCE	_____ _____
SUPPORTING SENTENCE	_____ _____
SUPPORTING SENTENCE	_____ _____
CLOSING SENTENCE	_____ _____

Draw your subject.

R1155 ISBN: 978-1-4877-0442-1 © On The Mark Press

LET'S TRY A FEW PARAGRAPHS:

TOPIC	How to make pizza.
TOPIC SENTENCE	_____ _____
SUPPORTING SENTENCE	_____ _____
SUPPORTING SENTENCE	_____ _____
SUPPORTING SENTENCE	_____ _____
CLOSING SENTENCE	_____ _____

Draw your subject.

R1155 ISBN: 978-1-4877-0442-1 © On The Mark Press

LET'S TRY A FEW PARAGRAPHS:

TOPIC	What I like to do in the summer.
TOPIC SENTENCE	
SUPPORTING SENTENCE	
SUPPORTING SENTENCE	
SUPPORTING SENTENCE	
CLOSING SENTENCE	

Draw your subject.

PARAGRAPH WORKSHEET

_____

title

_____

Topic sentence

_____

Detail 1

_____

Detail 2

_____

Detail 3

_____

Detail 4

_____

Detail 5

_____

Concluding sentence

_____

    R1155 ISBN: 978-1-4877-0442-1

WRITING CENTRE

If you want your students to write, you have to promote writing. Writing for a child who is not well equipped, does not understand how-to, has too many ideas and is not sure how to put them down on paper will find it very frustrating. Create a **Writing Centre** within your classroom. It won't take you too much time to set up and you can use many recycled items to lure your students into creative writing. Make it fun rather than making it a chore and they will be asking you if they can write more!

You will need:

• an area or corner away from the main door.

• a few tables and chairs. Foot stools are great too so they don't get distracted with dangling feet.

• Use prompts and posters with transition words, connecting words, adjectives etc. and change them regularly to inspire them. Have a few dictionaries too such as English, Rhyming, and Thesaurus.

• On the tables, display different types of paper available for writing. Have on hand recycled paper for their drafts and for their good copy stationary, index cards, lined paper, coloured-paper, writing pads, envelopes, postcards, greeting cards, stickers and stamps.

At the centre place a laptop/computer for publishing on the web.

Include a tray/box with writing examples such as: a map, a flyer, a menu, a recipe, a craft, a poem etc.

Include a tray/box where the students can put their drafts when they feel it is ready for editing.

• Include a tray/box of various worksheets such as those found in this book to allow children to practise, refresh and learn at their own pace.

• Allow each student to have access to the Sentence Creator in this book. Let them take their imagination and write, write and write!

• Make a big deal of published pieces. Create a Reading Corner with lots of their stories. Upload them to the school's web sites. Have a monthly Author's Tea to celebrate the wonderful writings your students create. If you make a big deal of it – they will reward you with interest and many, many stories!

PARAGRAPH OF THE WEEK

Included in this book are 40 weeks of paragraph writing prompts. You can chose how you will use these prompts but here are a few suggestions.

1. Photocopy all 40 weeks. Laminate the pages and cut out the prompts individually and put all 200+ prompts in a container and add it to your Writing Centre. Have students pick from the container and write a paragraph.

2. Photocopy all 40 weeks. Laminate the pages and cut the prompts individually and put all 200+ prompts in a container and add to your Writing Centre. Have students pick from the container and write a paragraph on a daily basis as you would do in a station within your Daily 5.

3. Use the Subjects given and have the student choose one paragraph idea and write one paragraph a week.

4. Use the Subjects given and assign one Subject a week. Have your students write a paragraph at night as homework as you would assign the nightly Reading Log.

5. Use the Subjects given and separate your students into small groups and have a friendly competition on how diverse the paragraphs can be within the same subject.

6. Use the Subjects given and match them to your curriculum. Every once in a while have your students pick the subject and the possible writing prompts to create a connection to the subject and paragraph writing ideas.

The Subjects and matching paragraphs are not numbered therefore you can choose the right subject according to events, timeline and holidays happening within your school year and establish a connection to your set curriculum.

Each Subject has 5 paragraph writing ideas. Each Subject has a blank one to allow you or your students the possibility to add another one.

   R1155 ISBN: 978-1-4877-0442-1 © On The Mark Press

PARAGRAPH OF THE WEEK

Subject: <u>Animals</u>

<u>Animals</u>: baby animals

<u>Animals</u>: Toys for animals

<u>Animals</u>: Farm animals

<u>Animals</u>: Should we have zoos?

<u>Animals</u>: Scary animals

<u>Animals</u>:

R1155 ISBN: 978-1-4877-0442-1 © On The Mark Press

Subject: <u>All About Me</u>

<u>All About Me</u>: Facts about me

<u>All About Me</u>: My family

<u>All About Me</u>: My school

<u>All About Me</u>: My favourite thing to do

<u>All About Me</u>: My pet (or want to have a pet)

<u>All About Me</u>:

R1155 ISBN: 978-1-4877-0442-1 © On The Mark Press

PARAGRAPH OF THE WEEK

Subject: <u>Super Heroes</u>

<u>Super Heroes</u>: My favourite super hero

<u>Super Heroes</u>: If I were a super hero, I would

<u>Super Heroes</u>: Create your own Super Hero – what powers would he/she have?

<u>Super Heroes</u>: The most funniest Super Hero is

<u>Super Heroes</u>: Super Heroes do great things

<u>Super Heroes</u>:

PARAGRAPH OF THE WEEK

Subject: <u>Storms</u>

<u>Storms</u>: Stuck inside during a snow storm

<u>Storms</u>: Caught outside during a rain storm

<u>Storms</u>: Prepare for a storm

<u>Storms</u>: Missing school because of the weather

<u>Storms</u>: Have you ever been in a wind storm?

<u>Storms</u>:

R1155 ISBN: 978-1-4877-0442-1 © On The Mark Press

PARAGRAPH OF THE WEEK

Subject: <u>My Town/City</u>

<u>My Town</u>: Where do I live?

<u>My Town</u>: Activities within my town

<u>My Town</u>: Shopping in my town

<u>My Town</u>: People within my town

<u>My Town</u>: The Best Things About My Town

<u>My Town</u>:

Subject: <u>My Family</u>

<u>My Family</u>: My Grandparents

<u>My Family</u>: My Siblings

<u>My Family</u>: My Parents

<u>My Family</u>: My Family Tree

<u>My Family</u>: The Most Important Thing About My Family

<u>My Family</u>:

R1155 ISBN: 978-1-4877-0442-1 © On The Mark Press

Subject: <u>My Favourite Pet</u>

<u>My Favourite Pet</u>: My Dog

<u>My Favourite Pet</u>: My Cat

<u>My Favourite Pet</u>: My Wild Pet

<u>My Favourite Pet</u>: My Pet Dinosaur

<u>My Favourite Pet</u>: My Pet Rock

<u>My Favourite Pet</u>:

R1155 ISBN: 978-1-4877-0442-1 © On The Mark Press

Subject: <u>All About SPACE</u>

<u>All About SPACE</u>: My Favourite Planet

<u>All About SPACE</u>: The Milky Way

<u>All About SPACE</u>: The Best Astronaut

<u>All About SPACE</u>: I Love Rockets

<u>All About SPACE</u>: N.A.S.A.

<u>All About SPACE</u>:

R1155 ISBN: 978-1-4877-0442-1 © On The Mark Press

PARAGRAPH OF THE WEEK

Subject: <u>Transportation</u>

<u>Transportation</u>: My Favourite Car Ride

<u>Transportation</u>: I Have My Airplane Tickets

<u>Transportation</u>: I Will Cruise on a Boat

<u>Transportation</u>: The Bus Ride to School

<u>Transportation</u>: Have You Ever Taken the Train?

<u>Transportation</u>:

Subject: <u>Cooking</u>

<u>Cooking</u>: The Perfect Ice Cream Sunday

<u>Cooking</u>: My Favourite Pizza

<u>Cooking</u>: The Worst Snack EVER!

<u>Cooking</u>: I Can Make My Own Breakfast

<u>Cooking</u>: Making a Smoothie

<u>Cooking</u>:

R1155 ISBN: 978-1-4877-0442-1 © On The Mark Press

Subject: <u>Fun Games</u>

<u>Fun Games</u>: How to Play Crazy 8s

<u>Fun Games</u>: Do You Know How To Play BINGO?

<u>Fun Games</u>: My Favourite Video Game

<u>Fun Games</u>: Let's Rock-Paper-Scissors

<u>Fun Games</u>: I Would Love to Get The Board Game

<u>Fun Games</u>:

R1155 ISBN: 978-1-4877-0442-1 © On The Mark Press

Subject: <u>I Love Being in The Kitchen</u>

<u>I Love Being in The Kitchen</u>: Write Your Favourite Recipe

<u>I Love Being in The Kitchen</u>: How to Set the Table

<u>I Love Being in The Kitchen</u>: How I Help Mom in the Kitchen

<u>I Love Being in The Kitchen</u>: Don't forget the Grocery List

<u>I Love Being in The Kitchen</u>: How to Use an Appliance

<u>I Love Being in The Kitchen</u>:

R1155 ISBN: 978-1-4877-0442-1 © On The Mark Press

PARAGRAPH OF THE WEEK

Subject: <u>Going to the Circus</u>

<u>Going to the Circus</u>: My Favourite Act at the Circus

<u>Going to the Circus</u>: The Circus is a Good Thing or a Bad Thing?

<u>Going to the Circus</u>: Send in the Clowns

<u>Going to the Circus</u>: Food at the Circus

<u>Going to the Circus</u>: At the Circus I feel …

<u>Going to the Circus</u>:

Subject: <u>Giving Thanks</u>

<u>Giving Thanks:</u> To My Parents

<u>Giving Thanks:</u> To My Teacher

<u>Giving Thanks:</u> To My Best Friend

<u>Giving Thanks:</u> To My Bus Driver

<u>Giving Thanks:</u> To My Favourite Actor/Actress

<u>Giving Thanks:</u>

R1155 ISBN: 978-1-4877-0442-1 © On The Mark Press

PARAGRAPH OF THE WEEK

Subject: <u>Birthday Wishes</u>

<u>Birthday Wishes</u>: Do I Celebrate Birthdays?

<u>Birthday Wishes</u>: Birthday Cake

<u>Birthday Wishes</u>: Birthday Party Games

<u>Birthday Wishes</u>: Most Memorable Gift Given to Me

<u>Birthday Wishes</u>: Most Memorable Gift I Have Given

<u>Birthday Wishes</u>:

R1155 ISBN: 978-1-4877-0442-1 © On The Mark Press

Subject: <u>Signs of Spring</u>

<u>Signs of Spring</u>: Sowing Seeds

<u>Signs of Spring</u>: Melting Snow

<u>Signs of Spring</u>: Animals in Spring

<u>Signs of Spring</u>: Preparing for Spring

<u>Signs of Spring</u>: Holidays During Spring Time

<u>Signs of Spring</u>:

   R1155 ISBN: 978-1-4877-0442-1 © On The Mark Press

PARAGRAPH OF THE WEEK

Subject: <u>Summer Fun</u>

<u>Summer Fun</u>: My Favourite Place to Swim

<u>Summer Fun</u>: Let's Go On a Picnic

<u>Summer Fun</u>: Our Day At The Beach

<u>Summer Fun</u>: Summertime Fun Activities

<u>Summer Fun</u>: I Love Camping!

<u>Summer Fun</u>:

R1155 ISBN: 978-1-4877-0442-1 © On The Mark Press

Subject: <u>Sports</u>

<u>Sports</u>: Playing Soccer

<u>Sports</u>: Hockey – What's a Hat Trick?

<u>Sports</u>: Baseball – 3 Strikes You're Out!

<u>Sports</u>: One Day I Will Get My Black Belt

<u>Sports</u>: What's a Tailgate Party?

<u>Sports</u>:

 R1155 ISBN: 978-1-4877-0442-1 © On The Mark Press

PARAGRAPH OF THE WEEK

Subject: <u>Special Days</u>

<u>Special Days</u>: Mother's Day

<u>Special Days</u>: Father's Day

<u>Special Days</u>: Grandparents' Day

<u>Special Days</u>: St-Valentine's Day

<u>Special Days</u>: Groundhog Day

<u>Special Days</u>:

Subject: <u>Sight Seeing</u>

<u>Sight Seeing</u>: Going on a Motorcycle Ride

<u>Sight Seeing</u>: Going to the Museum

<u>Sight Seeing</u>: Visiting a New Park

<u>Sight Seeing</u>: Let's go to a Theme Park

<u>Sight Seeing</u>: I Want to See a Show

<u>Sight Seeing</u>:

R1155 ISBN: 978-1-4877-0442-1 © On The Mark Press

Subject: <u>First Week Of School</u>

<u>First Week Of School</u>: Describe Your New Classroom

<u>First Week Of School</u>: Talk About Your Reading Buddy

<u>First Week Of School</u>: New School Year Resolution

<u>First Week Of School</u>: Summer Was Fun

<u>First Week Of School</u>: Activities You Look Forward to

<u>First Week Of School</u>:

Subject: <u>I Love Fall</u>

<u>I Love Fall</u>: Signs of Fall

<u>I Love Fall</u>: Labour Day

<u>I Love Fall</u>: Pumpkin Time

<u>I Love Fall</u>: Thanksgiving

<u>I Love Fall</u>: Harvest Season

<u>I Love Fall</u>:

R1155 ISBN: 978-1-4877-0442-1 © On The Mark Press

PARAGRAPH OF THE WEEK

Subject: <u>Halloween</u>

<u>Halloween</u>: My Favourite Costume

<u>Halloween</u>: A Scary Night

<u>Halloween</u>: Trick or Treat

<u>Halloween</u>: My Favourite Halloween Candy

<u>Halloween</u>: Orange and Black

<u>Halloween</u>:

R1155 ISBN: 978-1-4877-0442-1 © On The Mark Press

Subject: <u>December Holidays</u>

<u>December Holidays</u>: Bodhi Day

<u>December Holidays</u>: Hanukkah

<u>December Holidays</u>: Pancha Ganapati

<u>December Holidays</u>: Kwanzaa

<u>December Holidays</u>: Christmas

<u>December Holidays</u>:

R1155 ISBN: 978-1-4877-0442-1 © On The Mark Press

Subject: <u>Let it Snow</u>!

<u>Let it Snow!</u>: Fun in the Snow

<u>Let it Snow!</u>: Preparing For a Winter Blizzard

<u>Let it Snow!</u>: The Night The Power Went Out

<u>Let it Snow!</u>: First Signs of Snow

<u>Let it Snow!</u>: Let's Build a Snowman

<u>Let it Snow!</u>:

Subject: <u>I Love to Read</u>

<u>I Love to Read</u>: My Favourite Author

<u>I Love to Read</u>: The Kind of Books I Love to Read

<u>I Love to Read</u>: The Kind of Books I Don't Love to Read

<u>I Love to Read</u>: My Reading Buddy

<u>I Love to Read</u>: I Can Read Aloud

<u>I Love to Read</u>:

R1155 ISBN: 978-1-4877-0442-1 © On The Mark Press

PARAGRAPH OF THE WEEK

Subject: <u>Mother Nature</u>

<u>Mother Nature</u>: Water

<u>Mother Nature</u>: Wind

<u>Mother Nature</u>: Fire

<u>Mother Nature</u>: Earth

<u>Mother Nature</u>: Rain

<u>Mother Nature</u>:

Subject: <u>My Chores</u>

<u>My Chores</u>: My Indoor Chores

<u>My Chores</u>: My Outdoor Chores

<u>My Chores</u>: Helping Someone

<u>My Chores</u>: Pay it Forward

<u>My Chores</u>: Chores That Make Me Proud

<u>My Chores</u>:

R1155 ISBN: 978-1-4877-0442-1 © On The Mark Press

PARAGRAPH OF THE WEEK

Subject: <u>Music</u>

<u>Music</u>: My Favourite Musical Instrument

<u>Music</u>: My Favourite Band

<u>Music</u>: My Favourite Kind of Music

<u>Music</u>: My Favourite Song

<u>Music</u>: One Day, I Will Play ….

<u>Music</u>:

Subject: A Family Event

A Family Event: Told By Mom

A Family Event: Told By Dad

A Family Event: Told By The Baby in The Family

A Family Event: Told By the Family Pet

A Family Event: Told By a Fly on The Wall

A Family Event:

R1155 ISBN: 978-1-4877-0442-1 © On The Mark Press

PARAGRAPH OF THE WEEK

Subject: <u>If...</u>

<u>If ...</u> I could fly...

<u>If ...</u> I could be invisible...

<u>If ...</u> I was the Queen/King...

<u>If ...</u> I was a Spy...

<u>If ...</u> I never went to school...

<u>If ...</u>

R1155 ISBN: 978-1-4877-0442-1 © On The Mark Press

Subject: <u>The BEST Thing</u>

<u>The Best Thing</u>: My Best Friend

<u>The Best Thing</u>: The Best Toy

<u>The Best Thing</u>: 3–5 Best Things About Me

<u>The Best Thing</u>: The Best Thing in My Life

<u>The Best Thing</u>: My Best Day

<u>The Best Thing</u>:

     R1155 ISBN: 978-1-4877-0442-1 © On The Mark Press

PARAGRAPH OF THE WEEK

Subject: <u>I Remember …</u>

<u>I Remember …</u>: When I Was 2

<u>I Remember …</u>: When I Was in Kindergarten

<u>I Remember …</u>: When I Was on Vacation

<u>I Remember …</u>: Losing my First Tooth

<u>I Remember …</u>: Getting My First Pet

<u>I Remember …</u>:

PARAGRAPH OF THE WEEK

Subject: <u>Weekend Activities</u>

<u>Weekend Activities</u>: Going On A Sleepover

<u>Weekend Activities</u>: Going Camping

<u>Weekend Activities</u>: Going to the Theme Park

<u>Weekend Activities</u>: Going to the Movies

<u>Weekend Activities</u>: Going Fishing

<u>Weekend Activities</u>:

R1155 ISBN: 978-1-4877-0442-1 © On The Mark Press

Subject: <u>Secret (Shhh!)</u>

<u>Secret (Shhh!)</u>: Do You Know A Secret?

<u>Secret (Shhh!)</u>: A Secret Cave

<u>Secret (Shhh!)</u>: A Secret Hide Out

<u>Secret (Shhh!)</u>: My Secret Friend

<u>Secret (Shhh!)</u>: A Secret Secret

<u>Secret (Shhh!)</u>:

R1155 ISBN: 978-1-4877-0442-1 © On The Mark Press

Subject: <u>Feelings</u>

<u>Feelings</u>: Be Happy

<u>Feelings</u>: When I am Sad

<u>Feelings</u>: I Love to Laugh

<u>Feelings</u>: What Makes Me Giggle

<u>Feelings</u>: I Get Cranky When I …

<u>Feelings</u>:

   R1155 ISBN: 978-1-4877-0442-1 © On The Mark Press

PARAGRAPH OF THE WEEK

Subject: <u>ROBOTS</u>

<u>Robots</u>: My Recycled Robots-Stays

<u>Robots</u>: My Imaginary Robot

<u>Robots</u>: Rocky Robot

<u>Robots</u>: One Day Robots Will

<u>Robots</u>: The Best Robot

<u>Robots</u>:

Subject: <u>Food</u>

<u>Food</u>: My Favourite Lunch

<u>Food</u>: My Favourite Supper

<u>Food</u>: My Best Dessert

<u>Food</u>: I Love BBQs

<u>Food</u>: My Favourite Restaurant

<u>Food</u>:

R1155 ISBN: 978-1-4877-0442-1 © On The Mark Press

Subject: <u>Going On A Trip</u>

<u>Going On A Trip</u>: Taking a Trip in the Future

<u>Going On A Trip</u>: Making a Time Capsule

<u>Going On A Trip</u>: Going in The Past

<u>Going On A Trip</u>: Dream

<u>Going On A Trip</u>: Creating a Time Machine

<u>Going On A Trip</u>:

R1155 ISBN: 978-1-4877-0442-1 © On The Mark Press

Subject: <u>Superstitions</u>

<u>Superstitions</u>: Are You Superstitious?

<u>Superstitions</u>: Good Luck Charms

<u>Superstitions</u>: A Magic Trick

<u>Superstitions</u>: My Favourite Magician

<u>Superstitions</u>: A Magical Slogan

<u>Superstitions</u>:

R1155 ISBN: 978-1-4877-0442-1 © On The Mark Press

PARAGRAPH OF THE WEEK

Subject: _____